PSYCHOANAL
AND MORAL

BY JOHN COWPER POWYS

SAN FRANCISCO :: PUBLISHED BY
JESSICA COLBERT :: MCMXXIII

E. & R. Grabhorn, Printers

PSYCHOANALYSIS AND MORALITY

BY JOHN COWPER POWYS

The importance of what is now called "Psychoanalysis" has hardly been fully realized even yet. But there are not wanting signs and tokens that seem to suggest that it may prove as drastic a turning-point in the history of the human mind as was the theory of Copernicus in the history of the heavens. For it throws such startling side-lights upon the nature of sex and man's relation to sex as to go a long way towards creating a complete revolution in our Western attitude to these things.

Morality has of course other aspects than the sexual one; but the deadly and dominating power of the sex-instinct in the human race is so overwhelming that the popular connotation of morality with sex-morality has enormous justification. It must not be supposed that this tremendous revolution in our moral ideas will take place as the direct result of psychoanalytical investigation. Things rarely work that way in human affairs; and this particular situation, just because it is connected with sex, has so many deep and mysterious ramifications that any simple and plausible account of it, on the more obvious lines of cause and effect, cannot for a moment be expected. It is indirectly and not directly that the corrosive influence of this new science is already being felt. Like some insatiable acid-solvent, destined to eat gradually, inch by inch, into the very rock-bottom of our convictions, this formidable invader trickles down to those mental depths little by little and by the most round-about channels. Its very insidiousness, so evasive and elusive to the touch, militates against any attempt to arrest its movement or to dam up and fortify the chinks and crannies of the threatened citadel.

The appearance of psychoanalysis upon what might be called "The Moral Stage" is in reality a phenomenon of the most far-reaching seriousness, with implications that carry their disturbing vibration into the very recesses of our notions of good and evil. What it actually seems to amount to, from a rough and ready philosophical perspective, is indeed nothing less than the first definite invasion by cold-blooded empirical Science of a domain that has hitherto been ruled and monopolized almost exclusively by custom and tradition. For though through innumerable ages, Science has criticized and analyzed the metaphysical and dogmatic assumptions of religion, there seems to have been a profound and mysterious inhibition at work preventing it from touching with its unprejudiced curiosity those more vital human susceptibilities that are moral rather than theological. Indeed the very fact that scientific and philosophical investigators have in their cosmological scepticism, have been forced to contend against so much official and popular hostility may itself have rendered them rather more than less anxious to remain in guiltless accord with the *moral* assumptions of the human race.

This is, in point of historic fact, what we almost universally find; our boldest metaphysical revolutionaries positively growing obscure and tedious in their desire to reassure the average man that in matters of morality, that is to say of sex-morality, they are at one with the traditional opinion. It would almost appear as though in return for each successive portion of conquered terrain snatched from cosmological dogma, some new and yet more subtle "apologia" had been found for the corresponding moral "imperative" left suspended in the air. Not but what there have been certain great exceptions to this tendency. Nietzsche had the "wickedness" and the "innocence" to indicate that the same sceptical analysis which menaces Christine doctrine might, if carried a little deeper, be found just as threatening to the moral system which emanates from that doctrine. And Nietzsche himself only reduced to

2

Apollonian clarity the yet deeper and more formidable doubts stumbled upon in the very abysses of the Christian spirit itself, by the Dionysian genius of Dostoievsky. The truth seems to be that just in proportion to the terrific and overpowering role played in human life by the sex-instinct, the human mind is more *touchy*, more explosive, more irrational, more penetrated with inhibition, in regard to analysis of what is *there* than in regard to any other debatable ground. Nietzsche's own exaggerated aphorisms on the subject of morality were made more reckless and less weighty by the very fact that it required a mental effort in himself of almost super-human violence to arrive at the required detachment. It was the fury of his reaction from conventional ethics, or rather the fury with which he tugged at the roots of conventional ethics—for his own temperament was poisoned with Christian scruples—that evoked those fantastic eulogies of "blond-beasts" of Napoleons and Borgias, which with almost comic irrelevancy disturb the magical beauty of his conclusions.

It has indeed been very unfortunate, as far as the interests of an unprejudiced moral "critique" are concerned, that the only really inspired prophet of large re-valuations in this important matter should have been so put to it to clear his own conscience of diseased humors that the strain of such cleansing perturbed the equanimity of his vision. For one has only to glance at current literature to see how the noble and tragic aberrations of this heroic victim of his own over-sensitive soul have encouraged vulgar and shallow minds to confuse the whole issue by their blundering misapprehensions.

Certainly it would be a poor achievement for scientific analysis if it turned the mind away from the subtle and impassioned thinking of lonely and persecuted supermen to drop it plumb-down into the drunken bestiality of rampaging philistines! And that really is the pass to which things have come. On the one hand we have the troubled and inhibited conscience of the average "good" man and "good" woman; and on the other the gross and barbarous

3

kicking-up-its-heels of a "blond beast," who has much more in common with the physiology of the stock-yard than with the romance of the primitive jungle.

It is into the midst of this "impasse" that Science— cold-blooded experimental Science—comes forward now, with the intention of investigating, of analyzing, of tabulating, the actual flora and fauna, so to speak, of this explosive and volcanic territory; so that it shall be known at last, at least by those who care to know, what kind of forces they are that quiver and jerk and vibrate there so spasmodically and blindly, and that reject with such irrational repulsion all intelligent approach.

It must not be supposed that the only aim of psychoanalysis is to heal the mentally disordered. The art of healing enters largely into it. In the processes of healing its most significant conclusions have been reached. Its most famous and authoritative exponents belong to the medical profession. But psychoanalysis is a science as well as an art; and its ultimate aim is the old familiar aim of all human philosophy, namely the attainment of that difficult and delicate adjustment between our intelligence and the mystery that surrounds it that we are in the habit of loosely referring to as "the truth."

The curious agitations and disturbances aroused in the popular mind by the idea of this particular science; the furtive and secretive interest it excites, the neurotic persons it attracts, the neurotic persons it violently repels, the hostility stirred up against it in quarters where the moral "status quo" is used as a cloak for all maliciousness —these things are themselves a proof of the extraordinary importance of this new philosophical adventure. And they are also a proof of how treacherous the elements are, with which this new science has to deal; so treacherous indeed that the very motives and impulses that propel the psychoanalyist himself are themselves no negligible part of the "perilous stuff" which it is his duty to analyze. It is a strange commentary upon the character of human intelligence that it is only after so many thousands of years of

4

trary, is the whole thing a stupid blunder, one of those fantastic and arbitrary inhibitions, by which humanity seems wilfully bent upon assassinating its own happiness?

That there should have ever appeared at all in the world the tyrannous idea that by the drastic suppression of certain pleasurable sensations we can attain higher levels of human consciousness is the thing to be wondered at. And do we actually attain such higher levels by such drastic suppression? That also is a question to be asked.

The answer of psychoanalysis to this latter query is clear and unmistakable. If we do attain such levels it is at the risk of morbid and violent reactions, carrying us back even beyond the normal starting point; back, by a terrible swing of the pendulum, into lamentable disorder. But even so, considering the astounding force of this great magnetic current and the incredible power that can be engendered by suppressing it, might it not be better, one might ask, to risk these individual lapses and reversions, and to continue blindly damming up this great stream, on the chance that average humanity may really reach by this means a higher, subtler, more finely-attuned level of life? And so we come back to the question, is this moral tendency, now at least two thousand years old, to regard sex-pleasures as in themselves evil, the answer to a faint prophetic whisper issuing from the heart of Nature herself, promising humanity, if it does achieve this miracle of suppression, incredible rewards of heightened consciousness and clarified vision? Or, is it from the beginning until now, no better than what the sceptical Anatole France considers it, a monstrous and fantastic blunder, an insane superstition, an infatuated side-tracking of the great interests of human civilization, an insult to Nature, an outrage to the dignity of man?

If it does really appear that it is towards this latter supposition that the conclusions of psychoanalysis point, we should be compelled to recognize that the divinist words yet spoken by human lips upon this bewildering planet contained among them certain false, dangerous, and de-

structive tendencies. Yes! we should be driven to admit that
in their extraordinary hostility to sex-pleasure and sex-in-
dulgence, the doctrines of Christ, carried to yet more morbid
lengths by the desperate genius of St. Paul, have inflicted
a fatal wound upon the legitimate happiness of humanity!

For the processes of this new science carry with them
implications and corollaries, far deeper and larger than
appear on the surface; implications that throw a sharp
and cutting ray of shameless light upon the whole Christianized morality of our Western nations. If it is true that
the tender and magical genius of the Founder of Christianity, reinforced by the more ambiguous energy of St. Paul,
has definitely guided humanity astray upon this great
point; if it is true that the alluring beauty of the mediaeval
ideal, touched by the high and penetrating charm of saint
and artist, of poet and martyr, has treacherously led poor,
easily-hypnotized human nerves into a reaction against the
very pulse of their reponse to life; why then—alarum— we
have been betrayed indeed. But it would seem that there
is no occasion for putting the contrast quite so starkly or
in quite so bare and brutal a form. Whether some deep sub-
conscious tendency in the stream of events, some "soul of
the world dreaming on things to come," moved humanity
to these heroic self-lacerations, or whether they were
brought about by a divine blunder, or by pure chance, the
fact remains that however cruelly individuals may have
suffered from this blighting of sex-pleasure by the deadly
shadow of sin, the aesthetic sense of the world, not to speak
of the enchanced sensitiveness of individual men and
women has been immeasurably enriched by this noble
and tragic illusion.

Cut out of art and philosophy and literature all that has
been evoked, of vibrant beauty and passionate loveliness,
by this colossal sex-supression, and consider the residue!
Who would not exchange the gay roguery, the wanton wit,
of a Voltaire, òr of a Heine, for one of those great mysterious single lines in Dante or in Milton which seem to
touch the very borders of the unutterable?

In recognizing, however, the aesthetic debt the world owes to sex-suppression, it must not be forgotten that the great poets of antiquity, depending upon natural human emotion alone, were able to reach levels at least as magical as those of Dante or Milton. There is certainly no sex-suppression in Homer; though the eternal tragedy of human fate is as nobly and magnanimously rendered there as anywhere in poetry.

It would be interesting to disentangle from the rich tapestry of Shakespeare's genius the particular imaginative effects that he attained solely by reason of the fact that he was, aesthetically at any rate, saturated by Christian humours. The more drastic our effort is—following the cold-blooded and dispassionate method of psycho-analysis—to extricate ourselves from the pressure of human tradition, the more does this amazing notion, lodged in the diseased conscience of our race, *that sex-sensation is sin*, startle and impress us.

Sometimes it presents itself to one's mind as the most remarkable human phenomenon in the whole historic evolution of our race. That it should ever have come about at all is indeed the wonder; when one considers the terrific power of the thing, its maddening and obsessing ubiquity! One would have supposed that man, this perplexed apparition between two eternities would have glanced shrewdly round him, tested the potentialities of his nerves and his senses, and deliberately decided to snatch whatever he *could* snatch of entrancing and thrilling happiness before he returned to his native dust. Not at all! Something within him or without him, some mysterious evolutionary power, or some self-lacerating insanity, has driven a wedge of inhibition deep down among those quivering nerves, poisoning them with an inexplicable hesitation. But what exquisite perfume and sweetness we owe to this poisoning of the "Innocence" of the senses?

One has only to envisage the rank, gross insensitive brutality of the later classic days, with their "savour of poisonous brass and metal sick" to realize how, like a breath of rain-drenched flowers, this new cult of chastity and loyalty has refreshed and subtilized human life.

A modern traveller in Rome, passing from the vast sun-burnt ruins of the Colisseum or the Baths of Caracalla into some little Early-Christian church, with its wistful carvings and ivory-white fragilities, fresh and tender as forest-ferns in moss-grown pools, cannot but feel that in this mysterious restraint there does lurk some secret wisdom not altogether divorced from the crafty wiles of great creative Nature!

And yet, against the beguiling provocation of such a contrast, we should do well not to forget that that "innocent" classic world, unconscious that sex-pleasure was sin, had its own method of purging the sense-besotted spirit of man.

Are there not passages in the great Platonic Dialogues, written long centuries before Saint Paul turned away from women, magically lovely in their high pure lights and tender shadows and capable still of lifting the human soul out of material grossness into translunar vision? And yet, many of these very passages are intimately bound up with one of the most sinful of those sexual perversities studied so cold-bloodedly by psychoanalysis! Is it fantastic to hazard the suggestion that all the way down the ages there have been fortunate solitary individuals here and there, who arrived by some happy instinct at a reconciliation between these two terrific urges; the urge to enjoy sex-pleasure and the urge to suppress sex-pleasure? Such lucky ones, we may fancy, approached the thing lightly, easily, indulgently, naturally, and attained a rare and subtle attitude towards it such as nowadays we find it very difficult to reach. Such persons, we may suppose, dealt with sex-pleasure as artists deal with some flexible and malleable material, moulding it into forms of beauty and freedom. And the rhythm of their sex-life was neither hurt by the ache of ill-advised restraint nor bleached and tarnished by the misery of cynical satiety. For indeed it does seem likely enough that what has only been possible hitherto under the pressure of supernatural illusion may become possible in the future by the refining and sensitizing of sex-pleasure by the sex-instinct itself. When once the idea that such sensations are *sin* has been completely erradicated from the bewildered and hyponotized human mind, it may well happen that a natural sex-rhythm will assert itself, exercising an informed and easy restraint upon reckless excess; a restraint of which the dominant motive has ceased to be morality and has become aesthetic sense, or even common sense.

These *names*, however, are so misleading! One can easily imagine a tiresome and absurd tyranny exercised in the name of "aesthetic taste" or any other grandiose imperative, that would be just as inimical to honest human happiness as the idea of sin!

The thing, in fact, occurs daily. New Aestheticism, as old morality "writ large" is able to put on just the same censorious airs as the other and provoke just the same hypocrisies and reactions.

What one cannot help hoping will by degrees lodge itself in the human brain is a natural and friendly attitude towards all sex-pleasure, an attitude not unmingled with something of that old poetic worship of sex as sex of which the ancient heathen cults were an instinctive expression.

The repulsive and odious vulgarity of our modern American attitude to sex-pleasure is flagrantly illustrated by the tone of our popular newspapers when any social lapse of this kind is dragged forth into the light. A queer torrent of emotion seems just then released wherein a half-comic, half-obscene sentimentality, gloating over its victims, mingles with a positive orgy of ethical vengeance, the brutality of which rises to the sadism of the pillory.

One can only suppose that the same electric vibrations in human nerves and the same perilous secretions in human glands which drove forth the ancient tribes of men to worship Dionysus upon his hilltops and Ashtoreth in her forest-groves express themselves now—in a form vulgarized and debased, in these comic-brutal malice-dances,

13

drunk with sentiment and cruelty, round the moralistic
lynching-post!

Psychoanalysis will deserve the gratitude of all sensitive
and generous spirits if, apart from everything else, it reveals the complicated wickedness of these persecutors of
sex-delinquents. It will show how in the bursts of blind
moral anger displayed by the average man and woman
when confronted by some sex-lapse in another person,
there surges up a boiling flood of suppressed envy and
jealousy and thwarted lust. It will show how almost all
moral indignation, where such lapses are concerned, is an
ambiguous and very questionable emotion. Encouraged
by the investigation of psychoanalysis our long-persecuted
sex-consciousness begins to gather itself together for a
tremendous revolt. Not that this revolt, as its momentum
increases, will lead to any startling or shocking excesses.
Such excesses, such orgies of unbridled eroticism will remain precisely where they are at present. They will remain
the peculiar monopoly of the troubled imagination of the
sex-suppressed mind with its consequent vehement reactions. But a change will undoubtedly come about,
whereby the particular inhibitions which have always been
the ambiguous and questionable element in Christianity
will relax their hold.

The essential secret of Christianity, its emphasis upon
tenderness and forgiveness as opposed to unrelenting
malice, will by degrees, one cannot but feel, disentangle
itself from this other thing. The increasing economic independence of women will doubtless do much to hasten this
consummation; and so far from its results being injurious
to the weak and the helpless, one of its very first effects
would be the diminishing of professional prostitution. It
is not to be supposed that "the oldest trade in the world"
would even then, much as one might wish it to do so, entirely disappear; but it would certainly lose a great deal
of the sinister furtiveness that so vastly increases its worst
aspects. Nor can it for a moment be dreamed that the
nobler instincts in humanity—the passion for beauty, the

pity for suffering, the heroic impulses towards loyalty and sacrifice—will grow dim and faint because the human joy in sex and the human pleasure of sex-sensation assume their rightful place. Sensitiveness will still be sensitiveness, imagination will still be imagination, generosity generosity, when this two-thousand-year-old adamantine chain, dark with the rusty blood of infinite cruelty, is struck at last from the beautiful limbs of Eros!

That it requires a superhuman effort to detach oneself from a moral imperative that has eaten into one's very bones does not imply that the effort will be in vain. There have always been great intelligences, like Rabelais and Montaigue, or in more modern times like Goethe and William Blake, who have resolutely dissociated themselves from this hypnotizing of our natural instincts and have surveyed the mysteries of sex with an unclouded eye. And what has been achieved in the past by supreme men of genius may be achieved in the future by quite simple and normal persons if these excellent psychoanalytical methods filter down into the intelligence of the crowd.

But will this filtering down among the masses of man, of a more philosophical and less conscience-stricken view, imply any increase of vulgar and insensitive brutality? On the contrary, it is possible to trace quite definitely the most odious excesses of our time to the very presence of this great taboo. For when a vulgar and coarse nature, haunted by a sense of immorality, does burst the barriers, the very feeling that it has already committed, so to speak, the unpardonable sin, drives it on to further and further recklessness. And it has nothing to fall back upon; no discipline in the art of pleasure, no training in the art of moderation, no cultivation of the aesthetic sense, no philosophical balance. Once out of the moralistic tradition it just "runs amok."

Between the curious sense of civilized discomfort that one feels in the presence of an ethical fanatic like Gladstone or Mazzini—not to speak of more bigoted puritans— and the civilized discomfort that one feels in the presence

15

of most modern debauchery there is little to choose. Possibly the former would be the more pleasant object of contemplation! But in reality the vulgar enjoyer of "orgies" is the product, the offspring, the creation, of this very champion of moral inhibitions. And, reversing the picture, the enjoyer of gross orgies creates in his turn the most plausible of all arguments in favour of our modern Savonorolas! Thus the pendulum swings; and between the devil of inhibition and the deep sea of roaring vulgarity all delicacy, all decency, all sensitiveness, all humane and civilized happiness, is lost and betrayed. If we grant that the object of human life upon this earth is a heightening and subtilizing of human consciousness in the presence of the ultimate mystery, it does surely seem just as ill-advised to close down the heavy portcullis of Sin upon the couriers and scouts of Sex as it does to plunge headlong, body and soul, into the erotic salt-marshes.

Perhaps the part played by Christian morals with their terrifying supernatural sanction *has* been necessary in the evolution of the race; if only to obtain the breathing space, the clear ledge of rock above the turbulent tide, wherefrom a new and more comprehensive view of things could be obtained. But it is also quite likely that "from now on" humanity were wise to stand upon its own feet in this matter, independent of any thoughts or fears or speculations about the invisible world. For it is not of course only Christian morality that we shall be driven to revalue if the psychoanalytical implications are followed to their natural conclusion. Christianity is only *one* of the great ascetic religions coming from the East that have hypnotized and are still hypnotizing our Western nations. What we are really confronted with, if we have the philosophical adventurousness equal to such a task, is nothing less than the *ascetic instinct*, the instinct to deny sex of the whole human race! There are other "saints" than Catholic saints and other ascetics than Christian ascetics; and we have against us in our attempt to return to the clear-eyed Hellenic scepticism in these things the whole ambiguous burden of those vast Oriental metaphysical systems which have done so much to poison the wells and spoil the sunshine for poor earth-born humanity. It is just here that we have the right to take hold of the scientific implications of psychoanalysis and use them as a "novum organum" of research in regard to the larger aspects of human psychology.

We are even enabled to turn the psychoanalytical searchlight upon the great inspired founders of metaphysical asceticism themselves and to note with a dispassionate scrutiny what the psychic vibrations were that drove them to their anti-sex crusades. We are further enabled to analyze the anti-sex reactions in ordinary humanity, that tendency to submit so quickly to conscience-stricken terrors and taboos, that "fear," as Lucretius calls it, "of the gods" that has played, so treacherously and constantly, into the hands of these great inspired ones. Among the chief causes of the fatal and hypnotizing influence of these "spiritual teachers" is the peculiar nature of the hero worship that they excite. This seems due to a very curious and not altogether noble instinct in the average man, namely his subconscious sexual jealousy and the relief he experiences from its removal. To the average man every *other man* is a potential sex-rival, and when a great moral teacher approaches, who has by his own effort towards purity put himself, so to speak, "out of the game" the average man instinctively displays his relief by a gesture of spontaneous gratitude and love towards such a self-obliterating competitor. And this subconscious delight in the handicapping of a powerful rival is further enhanced when, by the hypnotic teachings of such a renunciant, *other* men, other ordinary men, are also rendered "hors-de-combat." There is thus originated a very curious subconscious campaign among large numbers of average men for the elimination of sex-rivals, a campaign of which the individual himself is quite unaware, as, in his own nature, the terrible pendulum swings backward and forward between "fear of the gods" and desire for natural happiness.

17

Once put on the track of these psychological self-deceptions, and we hardly require the personal evidence of a Saint Paul or a Saint Augustine to become aware that some of the greatest saints have had in them the makings of the greatest sinners. The curious hero worship with which the average man regards the great ascetic is on a par with the same occult delight, expressive of a vast relief, with which the economic dispossessors of the poor welcome every form of mystical renunciation. And even with ordinary people there is a constant subconscious awareness that if a man ostentatiously parades his asceticism he will at once become a popular figure; because there will at once rally to his side all the equivocal satisfaction in his fellows that there is one rival the less on the field. And for this relief they will feel an intriguing mixture of gratitude and pity. So much for masculine admiration of a pure life!

When, however, we approach the feminine attitude to those things the subconscious tendency I refer to only applies when the virtuous object in question is a woman herself. Women have an even fiercer admiration for moral women than men have for moral men; and for a good reason! And reversely they have a far more savage indignation with women who have been discovered in immorality. To these they become tigresses of moral vengeance. But who can fail to have remarked the astounding and almost passionate indulgence displayed by the feminine heart towards vicious men? The avenging fury of a jealous woman is almost always directed towards her feminine rival while the erring male if not recklessly forgiven is punished without cruelty or malice. But in the case of the great ascetics, and indeed of all masculine ascetics the feminine attitude is very shameless and unconcealed. It is the frank expression of an irresistible sensual attraction. And this attraction is based upon the instinctive feminine knowledge that a condition of sexual restraint is a condition of suppressed desire. Round this suppressed desire they gather like butterflies round honeysuckle; for it is far more exciting to feminine nerves to tantalize and provoke

18

and adore the unattainable, than to yield to commonplace sensuality. There is also something infinitely seductive to feminine sensibility in the very suffering of these great joy-renouncing ones. Over the sterile sex-loveliness of these bruised and lacerated souls the desire of women hovers, like a rain-cloud over an enclosed garden, drawing into itself incredible perfumes.

Round the figures of all the great ascetics of history, women have gathered in half-virginal, half-maternal adoration. The ecstasies of this cult are not really as different as they appear from those other ecstasies of such as followed the outraged Dionysus, or the hurt Adonis, or that persecuted god "whose annual wound in Lebanon allured the Syrian damsels to lament his fate." For just because the sex-instinct in women is more diffused than in men and more intimately associated with every function of body and soul the great moral taboo is less of a restraint. They surmount it, they undermine it, they transmute it; they use it as a mask for infinite passional sublimations.

But it must not be supposed that the moral or immoral implications of psychoanalysis are exhausted in the mere enumeration of traditional sex-taboos. The fatal power of suppressed sex-libido, acting on the human mind with such overpowering force, is one more proof of the intimate association between the nerves and the intellect, between material vibrations and mental consciousness. Berman's glandular theories, supported by so much strange evidence, add still further weight, from another direction, to this recognition of the terrible dependence of mind upon body.

And what, one is bound to ask, is the philosophical corollary from all this scientific investigation of the chemistry of the human soul? In the first place, surely, there grows upon us a vaguely dawning sense that if sex-pleasure is no longer to be regarded as "sin," but as something to be taken humorously, indulgently, ironically, that other kind of moral *gravity*, the kind that makes it a duty to take God and Immortality seriously, may likewise be a tragic-

19

comic mistake! Carrying this suspicion, this obstinate questioning, a little further still, may we not begin to wonder if the human race in freeing itself from the great sex-taboo will not at one heroic jump o'erleap yet another "bank and shoal of time" and treat the whole situation, the whole queer business of being alive at all, in a less moralistic temper? Is it too wild a fancy to hazard the suggestion that the particular kind of philosophical austerity that lays the heaviest burdens upon our luckless species is almost always associated with a suppressed sex-life? And, on the contrary, that the boldest liberators of the human spirit have themselves lived, as far as sex is concerned, sane and unsuppressed lives? Socrates, Plato, Euripides, Lucretius, Rabelais, Shakespeare, Montaigne, Heine, Shelley, Goethe, Whitman, Dostoievsky—do we not feel conscious of a vague popular instinct which suspects them all of immorality as well as of impiety? Nor does the association of the idea of sex-sin with God and Immortality, far and deep though it goes, cover the whole field; because the sort of moral asceticism one has in one's mind finds many eloquent and even humorous defenders who reject the supernatural altogether and substitute for it such positive and definite conceptions as the betterment of the human race. But I think it does remain true that between a certain ethical austerity in the matter of sex and a certain philosophical austerity in the matter of the cosmic mystery there is a very close connection. And as these cold-blooded investigations into the nature of our sex-life undermine the emotional gravity of our sex-suppressions will they not also tend to undermine our corresponding emotional gravity with regard to the whole cosmic spectacle? And if this is the result of their analysis, must we regard such an issue as a deplorable disaster? I cannot think so!

When Goethe uttered the great words, "Earnestness alone makes life eternity" it is not necessary to suppose that he meant the particular kind of gravity which betrays the free spirit of the human race into the hands of the unimaginative dogmatist. It would be a wretched day for men and women when philosophical speculation became so "earnest" as to destroy the only really effective weapon we possess against the grotesque tyrannies of the universe —I mean the weapon *irony*. The especial sort of moral gravity which I might entitle "sex-suppression-gravity" does not allow much scope for this weapon. It leaves humanity disarmed in the presence of the universe; and it leaves the individual disarmed in the presence of humanity. If these modern investigations into the sex-labyrinth free us from the emotional tension that lies behind this unhappy temper they will earn our passionate gratitude.

It is the fear of sex-sensation as a tabooed thing that plays so subterraneously into the fear of cosmic criticism as a tabooed thing. A religious awe is evoked which must not be blasphemed. Sex is sacred and must be spoken of with bated breath. The universe is sacred and must be treated with ritualistic reverence. The sex-god must be propitiated. The universe-god must be propitiated. The human traditions that regulate these propitiations must be a very ark of sanctity. Humanity itself—poor hypnotized humanity—comes in too for *its* share of sacred awfulness; and the miserable individual, looking desperately around out of his world-trap, is forbidden even to smile at these solemn autocracies. That is the gist of the whole thing. The traditions that suppress sex-pleasure are hostile to individual happiness. The traditions that suppress cosmic-criticism are hostile to individual happiness. The traditional social-tyranny of the herd-instinct is hostile to individual happiness. It is always the individual who pays! By its scientific analysis of the dangers of sex-suppression this great new science of psychoanalysis has struck a splendid blow for individual relief. It has helped us to treat one grand taboo in a free ironic manner. It will doubtless help us to treat the others in the same way. It will encourage the individual to sink boldly back into his own soul and from that fortress to look around freely, sceptically, casually, carelessly, at the extraordinary universe into which "willy-nilly" he has been plunged. It will encourage the individual to gather his forces together in his own mind, to find out what his peculiarities, his tastes, his humours, really are; and then, to criticize his prison—for "Denmark" *is* a prison—with a whimsical irony that is independent of all preconceptions. It will encourage the individual to detach himself from the world-stream and to survey that stream with a clear and humorous eye. But at this point it is necessary to pause for a moment and indicate certain necessary qualifications.

The freedom I have been describing does not imply anything remotely approaching that "blond beast" brutality and violence and unscrupulousness which in his reaction from his own Christianized nerves the good Nietzsche recommended. *That* sort of liberty, the liberty of the predatory wild animal, the liberty to inflict discomfort and pain on others, is quite obviously just a philosophical license given to the strong at the expense of the weak, to the insensitive at the expense of the sensitive. Nothing could be more remote from the temper of this present treatise than such a hideous conclusion. *That* sort of liberty—the liberty of the strong to oppress and exploit the weak—is precisely what we contemplate now in the *existing* system of things. For all these grave traditions, religious, moral, philosophical, idealistic, which suppress and pervert so lamentably the frail, the sensitive and the "good," leave the tough and the insensitive quite unscathed. "Let the galled jade wince—our withers are unwrung."

Nietzsche's idea seems to have been that all these various taboos, hostile to individual happiness, were created by the weak "to keep the strong in awe." But Nietzsche himself answers himself when he hints at the doctrine of the Master-morality and the Slave-morality. For according to that method it is the strong and the crafty who have deliberately concocted these cunning idealistic philtres in order to pursue their rapacious path unimpeded. And this is precisely what we observe going on around us today. One had only to glance at the countenances of the average successful businessmen and the average successful politicians to become aware of the presence of a shrewd and sagacious hypocrisy. No! It is not the tough ones of the world who are the victims of these sex-taboos; it is the frail ones, the gentle ones, the sensitive ones; just the very ones in fact who never, however many taboos were lifted from them, could become brutal, cruel, violent, unscrupulous, or dangerous to others. Such popular terms of abuse as "decadent," "temperamental," "artistic," "degenerate," and so forth, are they terms that apply to the strong, as the world goes, or to the frail and the weak? Obviously to the frail and the weak! But these are the very terms with which the crafty Borgias—how *that* family would turn in their graves at the comparison!—of our modern commercial society stir up on the hearts of the mob the sex-jealousy-complex against the artist and the thinker. To return to the larger issues of the whole problem of psychoanalytical research, it must be allowed that the emphasis laid upon the intimate association between body and mind can easily be perverted into an argument for a gross and narrow materialism. Professor Berman's Glandular Theories, coming from a more rigidly physiological direction, might encourage this materialism still further.

Let us consider this dangerous possibility—*Materialism:* That too has become one of the word-bludgeons with which obscurantist persons, far more essentially "materialistic" than the thinkers they attack, seek to rouse the "our-idols-are-being-insulted" mood in the ignorant masses. If materialism means a human life devoid of imaginative vistas, then indeed it is the worst of evils. But if it means no more than a growing recognition of the mysterious potency of chemical and magnetic forces, it seems as though such a philosophical attitude must rather intensify than diminish an imaginative reaction to the universe. But perhaps the simplest use of the term is an implication *that there is nothing else in existence* except the material universe which we know so well, extending its time and space limits indefinitely in every direction. If this idea, the idea

23

of the possibilities of life, or existence, or reality, being rigidly confined to this particular spacial and temporal universe, is the result of scientific investigation into the psychology of the human mind—then indeed the case begins to grow serious. But there is not the least need for such a conclusion. It is always difficult to render clear in words the subtle metaphysical *necessities of thought* that make such a conclusion null and void; but any reader who takes the trouble to indulge in a little concentrated intro- spection will soon touch these unescapable considerations. For such turning inward will reveal the fact that there is something in the mind itself outside this spacial and temporal universe, something which has the power of con- templating this material universe *as if from the standpoint of another plane of existence.*

But quite apart from the revelations of metaphysical introspection, it may be remarked that ordinary reason, ordinary intelligence, ordinary common sense, whisper to us that it is *unthinkable* that the material universe of space and time *is* all of *Reality that there is.* Without any intro- duction of mysticism or spiritualism, or even of the higher mathematics, the mere common sense of the human mind refuses to accept a reality so narrow, so limited as this. For the mere extension of space without bound or end, and of time without bound or end, does not render this material universe any less narrow or imprisoning to the mind. The whole supposition is an insult to the infinite possibilities of life, to the infinite possibilities of Nature. Of course, there are millions of "planes of existence"; mil- lions upon millions of dream-worlds within dream-worlds!

The science of psychoanalysis, though its emphasis upon the connection between the mind and the bodily nerves is naturally dreaded by popular idealism, cannot be accused of limiting the possibilities of life to the spacial universe as we know it. Indeed its general tendency is to prepare the way for the most startling and formidable specula- tions. If sex-feelings, for example, go so far and so deep why should not the conscious individual mind which is the

24

theatre of such unfathomable conflicts, go further and deeper still? When one thinks of the unplumbed abysses of formless subconsciousness, into which the most powerful psychic telescope throws only a wavering glance, is not one tempted to envisage the individual soul—poor luckless victim of all these race-taboos!—as something larger and greater than has hitherto been guessed? Do not these recurrent revelations of deeper and deeper levels of obscure subconsciousness indicate that the individual soul sinks altogether out of the dream-level of the spacial universe into a region for which at present we have no chart? And not only does psychoanalysis suggest that there are unfathomable mine-shafts, so to speak, in the personal soul that reach out and beyond the sphere of material phenomena; it also seems to suggest that these mine-shafts of personality remain *individual* and do not lose themselves, as Oriental mysticism implies, in any over-soul or world-consciousness. To an intellect that remains sceptical about this hypothetical cosmic consciousness there is something peculiarly stimulating in the emphasis laid by these new methods upon the unfathomable difference between one soul and another soul. There is far too much vague chatter among loosely-thinking minds as to this "cosmic consciousness." What the individual soul really experiences as it sinks down into the depths of itself does not seem to be any submerging of its individual identity into "universal consciousness" or "universal life-force." These are convenient catch-words; but they do not at all express the actual facts of mental experience.

On the contrary, it would almost seem as though the individual soul of a man or a woman were a deeper and more real thing than the whole dream-world of the spacial and temporal universe that surrounds it and invades it. It would indeed be a remarkable result of psychoanalytical research if it encouraged us in the bold and startling speculation that individual personality is a more formidable reality than radio-magnetic, electro-chemical force! It may even turn out that the ancient classic mythologies, with their poetic "animism" or polytheistic "psychicism," approached more closely to the secret of the universe than our modern enumerations of unconscious sub-human energies. We talk lightly about chemical forces and life-forces. It would be indeed a startling reversion if the mysterious thing we endeavour to eliminate from our speculation—I mean the individual conscious soul—proved to be more powerful than any other vibrations or radio-explosions; proved to be in fact, the force that set these electric energies in motion! Psychoanalytical research would indeed have effected a formidable revolution, if, in its pursuit of the sex-element in the human mind, it found the human mind to be a much more important factor in the creation and destruction of dream-worlds than all the forces stored up in all of the atoms! After all our investigations into the chemistry of life it may yet turn out that the creator and destroyer of life, the thing that conceives life and absorbs life, is nothing less than the mind itself; the mind and the imagination! Thus, what we lightly call a by-product of life would turn out to be something which brought life itself into existence! When all "matter" is reduced to "motion" and all "motion" is reduced to radio-magnetic energy, it may suddenly appear that the "force-battery" which generates this mystery is nothing less than a conscious personal soul; the soul of a man, or of an animal, or of a plant; the soul, even, of a planet or of a star; and in this way human philosophy may come round full circle and what used to be called "anthropomorphism," and be regarded as the very height of absurdity, may be accepted as nearer the secret of things than any other solution. If psychoanalysis enables us to treat sex with ironic sagacity; if it enables us to free ourselves from the particular kind of world-awe that spoils the natural arbitrariness and independence of our individual protest; if it saves us from staggering too heavily under the weight of universe-worship or cosmic fetishism, if it delivers us, in fact, from that perturbing "fear of the gods" that might be named "providence-phobia," it will have done nobly by the

26

human race. And has it been thus left, one might ask, to this quietly obstinate cold-blooded science to play the part of the old original Serpent; whispering in our ears;—"Ye shall be as gods, knowing good and evil?" It does really almost amount to precisely that! For if the mind of a man or a woman is henceforth to be regarded as a vast universe in itself, full of deep black holes that descend into unfathomable mystery, why then, what was once the cosmic-panic becomes the self-panic; and we could "be bounded in a nutshell and count ourselves kings of infinite space, were it not that we have bad dreams!"

Psychoanalytical research does indeed act upon us indirectly as well as directly; and many of its indirect effects are the most formidable of all. By liberating us from the "mort-main" or dead hand of universe-worship, that huge and ultimate taboo, it sets free such creative and such destructive powers in the abysses of our own souls that we pause on the precipice-edge of the gulfs which are ourselves and shudder at our own supremacy.

Yes, we become as gods, knowing good and evil.

Not very great gods, it must be admitted! For "blastings, thwartings, and eclipses" still baffle and perplex us. But if the whole dream-world of ethereal chemistry yields even a little to the creative and destructive energy of our imagination; if by the use of a certain heavenly magic we can overcome the demons of our own mental inferno and create harmony where there was no harmony and peace where there was no peace; why then if we are not gods we are at least half-gods!

It is growing easier and easier to estimate the philosophical results of this modern taboo-breaking. And the most important result is that the individual is thrown back upon himself to take humorous and imaginative "stock" of the whole earthly situation. This "stock-taking" of the taboo-freed mind is the most important crisis in every individual soul. And it does not in the least necessitate a reversion to philistine brutality or orgiastic ruffianism. He that is gentle and sensitive will be gentle and sensitive still! But it does

27

imply that the beautiful-terrible panorama of life as it passes before us, so grotesque and so fantastic, so lovely and so obscene, will be observed with an eye unclouded by that curious instinct for "propitiating the universe" which is the residual ghost of all sex-superstitions. The man who refuses to propitiate the universe by accepting this or the other formula of ethical ponderousness does not necessarily become a jeering and shallow cynic. Such a man is not less aware, but much more aware, of the incredible mysteries that surround him on every side, of the high and sorrowful dignity of mortal passion, of the wistful loveliness of Nature, always withholding its secret, of the stern grandeur of human sacrifice, or the heart-breaking simplicity of human goodness. To free oneself from superstitious pedantry in these deep matters is not to become a gibing, thick-skinned, selfish clown. It is to become suddenly, freshly, vividly aware what an incredible chaos of wonder and horror, we have been born into, what appalling chasms open up beneath one's feet, what transporting horizons beckon and summon us towards unutterable paradises! To regard the naughty perversities of fate and chance with a whimsical eye, to regard one's own sex-obsessions and the sex-obsessions of others with humorous indulgence, to remain content with that natural human ignorance with respect to "what lies beyond" which is the note and temper of all the great un-hypnotized poets from Homer to Shakespeare, does not by any means imply a hurly-burly of gross self-indulgences or a hodge-podge of brutal buffooneries. Because one cannot be a Cardinal Newman there is no need to be a ————! Not for a moment does this refusal to be fooled by Nature into a totemistic solemnity mean that one becomes unsympathetic to the sufferings of the world. Voltaire was a person most singularly free from every superstition and yet the untiring fury of his struggle against man's cruelty to man never gave him a moment's rest. Whatever mental habits we may find it necessary to form, one habit must at all costs be avoided, the habit of taking for granted without question the particular gravity towards life which is the fashion of the age. For this gravity, though it may carry a philosophic mask, is directly connected with sex-touchiness and draws its "Theo-phobia" or "God-Terror" from sex-restriction. Not for nothing did the ancient poets associate Aphrodite with Ares, Venus with Mars; for it will almost always be found that a free, courageous, adventurous, and unhypnotized gaze into the mysteries of existence gathers its integrity and its happiness from some profound relaxation of the sex-taboo. Whether future psychologists will accept in their present form or not the particular theories connected with the myth of Oedipus and the even more suggestive and subtle theories connected with what is called "the inferiority-complex" and "the masculine protest," it remains that we have already learned from these great catch-words enough to make us realize how deeply-bedded and how unescapable our primordial sex-impulses are. Sex invades every thought we have, every animosity, every sympathy, every vague and obscure assertion of pride, every plunge into humiliation and self-effacement. How the recognition of all this enlarges the boundaries of our self-conscious world!

We begin to grow aware that the whole organism of our nerves and senses, as it stretches out its invisible tendrils towards the material objects that narrowed us, draws the method of its functioning from this one underlying urge. We actually do caress and possess with the obscure flow of our polymorphous "libido" every single external thing to which our attention is attracted. Or, if we do not lust after it, we reverse the movement, and shrink from it with sex-saturated loathing. The reaction of every living organism, animal and vegetable as well as human, towards the external world is penetrated by the two primordial impulses of hunger and desire; and one may actually question, without risk of any too far-fetched fantasy, whether hunger and thirst themselves are not mysteriously and intimately associated with sex. Certainly all human impulses that tend to the spending of energy are associated with it. For it would seem that the magnetic vibrations aroused in us by the effort of any labour, whether mental or physical, have a direct contact with the nerve-centres wherefrom sex-agitation proceeds. This is, above all, true in regard to aesthetic activity. Art and literature are so closely involved with sex-excitement that the rhythmic interchange between the systole and diastole of creative and receptive emotio—whether these opposites are found in the same person, or are incarnated in different persons—seems to have the most direct connection with male and female reciprocities. Wherever consciousness, even in the most rudimentary form, exists, that is to say in every species of individualized organism to which nature gives birth, there is an instinctive absorption of nourishment, which corresponds in its identity-lust with the instinctive rhythm of sex. This identity-lust, which brings the hunger-impulse and the sex-impulse so close together, might be described as an attempt to establish a complete inter-fusion between the organism that hungers and desires and the particular living body or chemical substance towards which its instinct is directed.

We are necessarily quite ignorant of the subjective reactions of non-human organisms; but without becoming fantastic in our speculation we may hazard a shrewd guess, following human analogy, that such subjective reactions in the sub-human world radiate very far and are by no means confined to the immediate sensations of satisfying hunger and the sex-impulse. It might be maintained that every living organism instinctively—like the human infant—stretches out every sense-nerve it possesses in order to satisfy its identity-lust by appropriating to itself as much of the external world, as it can reduce to submission to its mastery. The growing plant, for example, struggles through the expansion of its roots and leaves and petals to gratify its identity-lust by absorbing into itself whatever of the rain or dew or earth-mould it finds submissive to its domination. The beasts of the field, as with their sublime preoccupation they devour the grass, are

30

driven by the same instinct to reduce to material unity with themselves as much of the external universe as lends itself to their contemplative voracity. And behind the sex-functioning of both men and beasts and their blind pursuit of nourishment there stirs and moves the same centrifugal and centripetal force—this persistent identity-lust—aiming to bring about as complete an inter-fusion between themselves and the object of their desire, as the submissiveness of the object or the margin of their own satiety makes it possible to achieve. And the subjective reactions, even of sub-human creatures, cannot, we feel, be confined entirely to the immediate direct sensation, whether sexual or alimentative. There must be obscure margins of consciousness in their nervous systems which not only associate food and sex very intimately and closely; but associate both, in a vague and confused manner, with some mysterious correspondence or parallel to what, in us, is the aesthetic enjoyment of life.

We are thus led to the conclusion that in all forms of organic life upon the earth, from the lowest to the highest, there is a conscious instinct that associates the pursuit of nourishment with the pursuit of sex-delight and both of these things with that indefinable response to external objects to which our race gives the name of aesthetic pleasure. And when we come to analyze the precise sensations which we ourselves experience in the presence of the particular persons, or the particular works of art, or the particular scenes, that thrill us with the most complete harmony, we find that the realization of the identity-lust, by means of which we appropriate to ourselves and absorb into ourselves the object of our attraction, resembles not only the ecstasy of sex-satisfaction but the ecstasy of hunger-satisfaction. For it seems that what every human being obscurely struggles towards is nothing less than a polymorphous identity-lust, by means of which he at once possesses, devours, and aesthetically digests, as much of the unfathomable universe as he is able to appropriate to his desire. Carrying our analysis one step further, the question arises—is this synthetized identity-lust, composed of alimentative, sexual and aesthetic elements, limited in any particular way according to the individual nature of the organism which displays it? It seems that it is so limited. And at this point one has a right to make use of that suggestive term "Narcissism" with which psychoanalysts have provided us. For one might go so far as to maintain that what every man's and every woman's secret sub-consciousness seeks is nothing less than a diffused reproduction in the objective world of what they are subjectively in themselves. A rapacious and carnivorous sub-consciousness, whose psychic chemistry is crude and coarse, inevitably directs its identity-list to a certain reciprocal coarseness and crudity in the surrounding cosmos. On the other hand a gentle and fastidious sub-consciousness instinctively directs its "libido" towards a corresponding gentleness and evasiveness in the same cosmos.

In every human being there will be found some particular atavistic reversion to the vegetable-world, or the bird-world, or the fish-world, or, on the other hand, to the animal-world, whether carnivorous or the reverse. And beyond and below these obvious differences in man's identity-lust, there will be found certain strange occult reciprocities, suggestive sometimes of nothing less remote than planetary or even stellar influences.

The inherent Narcissism of our identity-lust can easily be tested in a thousand interesting and curious ways. We instinctively select among objects of food, for example, those which answer in some mysterious manner to the secret chemistry of our sub-conscious souls. We are drawn towards, or repelled by, certain fabrics and substances, certain soils, certain earth-formations, certain minerals, trees, plants, certain atmospheres and climates. And over, and over again, the outward and apparent texture of our nature, its conscious pose or mask to the world, is most quaintly refuted and exposed by these deeper, more instinctive preferences. The great Nietzsche, for example, for all his eloquence about "frightfulness" reveals the inherent fragility and refinement of his subconscious nature by his childish greed for honey in the honey-comb! A man or a woman who is obscurely thrilled, beyond their own comprehension, by certain effects of twilight, of mist, of faint grey shapes of clouds, of thin light-falling rain, will be discovered to have an illusive and a drifting soul, sub-human and elemental, such as very likely completely contradicts the cynical assumed countenance with which such an one confronts the world! But the best evidence of this peculiarity of the soul may be found in a very simple manner. Who has not remarked among the jostling crowds upon the pavements of our cities the extraordinary eye-encounters that go on between passers-by? These are not only signals of obscure attraction and repulsion. They are signals of unfathomable malice and love, of abysmal hatred and tenderness, of world-deep mockery and pity. And how does our identity-lust work among these pavement encounters?

It instinctively draws to itself those among the passers-by whose psychic chemistry resembles its own and it instinctively smites with a blind cerebral hostility those of antipodal ingredients whose least glance is a stinging challenge. One frequently surprises upon another human countenance, thus casually encountered, a look, which if it has any meaning at all, has the meaning—"you great lubber" —"you wretched little monkey"—"I'd like to smack your face; smack your face!"

And what is the origin of this curious emotion?

Nothing less than the quick instinctive recognition that the chemistry of this particular person's soul blocks the path of our indentity-lust and flings it back upon itself outraged and ridiculed. And why does it do this? Because in this particular encounter *we* find no trace of ourself and the other person finds no trace of *himself*. Both identity-lusts are insulted and mocked. Both come up against an adamantine wall.

The reason why so many love-affairs end disastrously is

33

that they are *specialized* love-affairs—that is to say, they represent a relation between the lovers which is only narrowly and functionally sexual, not universally and cosmically sexual. For a love-affair to be lasting, each lover must find in the other a sex-appeal that far transcends the mere functional urge. They must find something in the object of their desire that corresponds to their choice in all these other occult reciprocities. The person must represent the preferred climate, the preferred scenery, the preferred food, the preferred fabrics, substances, materials, elements! In other words the object of love, in order to retain the emotion, must be a sort of "microcosm" of that whole cosmos of preferences to which the identity-lust of the lover is drawn. And when these preferences are analyzed they will turn out to be nothing less than a diffusion throughout the whole chemical and mental universe of a projected reproduction of the lover's own sub-conscious nature! Thus what all lovers seek is nothing more or less than a objective shadow of their hidden soul, materialized and substantiated.

What looks like the appeal of "opposites" is a misleading illusion, the only justification of which is the pleasure we derive from finding ourselves mirrored and echoed in the very direction where we anticipated most resistance— thus we enjoy that likeness beneath difference which is the zest of all sexual attraction.

The moralistic taboo which stigmatizes as "sin" all sex-sensation not duly licensed by the community is in reality a deadly iron trap shut down on the actual living growth of a human soul. For, as the soul expands, its identity-lust becomes its means of contact with earth, air, water, and all that is. Thus one may note how the wretched unhappiness of human beings deprived of sex-satisfaction consists in something being taken from their food, something from the air they breathe, something from the thrill of the evening and the morning, something from the magical procession of the seasons, something from the spectacle of life and death.

34

Something—but not all!

For great creative Nature is kinder than human society; and while men and women breathe they find some answer, some response, to what I have named the identity-lust, but what in reality is the soul's search for "that imperial palace" of its own projection diffused throughout the universe!

Nor must it be forgotten that just as a too rigid taboo in these matters "hurts the poor creatures of earth", so also does the waste of disordered indiscrimination deaden and atrophy the sweet magic of life. The real argument against brutal and indiscriminate eroticism is not that it offends the gods of chastity but that it drives away the gods of happiness. For the more close we find the association to be between "the pleasure which there is in life itself" and the sex-sensation, the more does it become clear that a certain wisdom and refinement in these things cannot be sacrificed if we are to reach a really vivid and subtle consciousness of what it is to be born into this strange world!

When one looks below the surface of the foaming whirl-pools of emotional cross-currents that confuse the main issues today, one recognizes two great evolutionary changes—*first*, the relaxing of religious and moral tradition; and second, the economic independence of women.

Quite apart from psychoanalysis, which, after all, is itself only a scientific concentration of certain modern mental reactions, these two main tendencies—the relaxation of moral tradition and the emancipation of women—must be regarded as intimately associated with one another. Since every single one of these traditional customs of the race, social, political, moral and religious, has been made by man rather than by woman, it seems inevitable that with the growing independence of women all these man-made customs will be overhauled and revised. And what will be the effect upon sex-morality of this feminine revolution? Surely, it will be in the direction of a less drastic, a more relaxed and more natural regime!

Of course, when one contemplates the emotional violence

35

of the injured female partner in any especial case of sex-aberration, one might easily be tempted to assume that the effect of women's accession to liberty and power would mean an immediate tightening of the reins. And this view of the case might find further support in the judicial eccentricities of what is called "the unwritten law." But one has to look deeper into life and further afield than the pseudo-legal stage of these melodramatic comedies. Such explosions of sex-wrath belong to the category of moral lynchings and introduce all manner of erotic mob-suppressions which complicate the situation.

Women, as well as men, suffer from the crowd-complex; and are betrayed into moods and feelings quite contrary to their individual unperverted instinct. One has to look below these violent reversions to tribal-taboos to detect the real movement of the undertide of feminine psychology. Crimes of jealousy, on both sides, are committed under the present regime; and will be committed, one fears, under any regime.

But the new element in the situation, springing from the growing economic detachment of women from men, will by degrees shift the pressure of responsibility so that it no longer falls upon men alone. It seems indeed that it will fall with an increasing weight upon women rather than upon men. And it is from this shifting of the burden of sex-responsibility that the saner and wiser human attitude to these things may actually emerge. Imagine for a moment—and it is not unimaginable—a state of society in which the whole choice and discrimination in sex-affairs were left to the instinctive decision of women; not of women as a mob, drunk with sentimental tribal vodka, but of women as individuals. Is it to be supposed thàt the particular kind of superstitition we have been discussing would remain unchanged? It is indeed likely enough that all the way down the ages, woman's sane and natural instincts in these things have been twisted and perverted by man's extravagant asceticism, struggling with his extravagant satyrishness.

36

Perhaps if the truth were known there isn't a woman in the world who in her secret heart does not feel "that man's moral codes are grotesque and artificial." It is certainly true that when it comes to paying the price for both the ascetic's and the profligate's departures from the wisdom of our mother, the earth, women have been the ones to pay it most heavily. Psychoanalysis throws the influence of woman as a mother into a very searching light. Has it nothing to say about woman as an accomplice in love-making? Unfortunately all the greater psychoanalysists are of the male sex. But here, as in other branches of human thought, the time is surely at hand when some philosopher-woman will prove capable at last of articulating what has never yet been articulated—the real nature of woman's un-hypnotized reaction to the mystery of life. And when that time comes, for women remain much closer to Nature in matters of sex than men, it may well happen that a point of view will be brought into prominence sufficiently devastating both to the moralist and the ruffian! It may even happen that under the influence of such a point of view, at present concealed from us by women's philosophical inarticulateness, the desirable rhythm in these difficult matters will approach perceptibly nearer. What precise form this rhythm, this balance, this equation will take, even as an ideal, is not easy to say.

But one thing we *are* able to say about it; it will relax in unexpected directions the moralistic burdens that oppress us now. Though it is only likely enough that with new liberty, new chains of another metal will appear and new world-traps will be set. For the human race, whether ruled by men or by women, will deliver from oppression every kind and species of victim before it delivers, if it ever delivers, the *individual man* and the *individual woman!*

For after all, it does most woefully remain that the interests of the individual are not the interests of the race; any more than, as far as we can see, are the interests of the race the interests of the universe.

It seems as though in every human being there were a

37

race-instinct that conflicts with the personal instinct; and so touchy and sensitive to outrage is this race-instinct, that it sometimes might be supposed that *it* also possessed some strange "sex-libido" of its own, a sort of impersonal world-lust, seeking to create super-human offspring out of the dark matrix of the indetermined future! We are indeed, in these devious sexual impulses, strangely complicated and entangled.

For not only is our attraction mingled with curious repulsion, as far as the opposite sex is concerned, but we are forced to recognize that we possess elements of both sexes in our own nature. There is a man in every woman who derives a subtle masculine pleasure in "seducing" his other-self. There is a woman in every man who derives a subtle feminine pleasure from being "seduced" by her other self. We are all, in some degree or another, bi-sexual in our divided impulses; and in many respects it might be said that in the eternal human duality between body and soul, the body plays the part of a mysterious passive odalisque, whose secret, deep as nature herself, allures its companion-soul to perpetual creation and destruction. It is impossible to deny the epithet "sexual" to those mysterious wrestlings and strugglings that go on in the twilight of so many mental relations between man and man and woman and woman. One is cajoling, ensnaring, caressing; and one is responding with some obscurely hypnotized helplessness or some yet more obscurely hypnotized baffled anger.

It hardly ever happens that two human beings of the same sex are brought into close relationship without one of them being in some mysterious way vampirized by the other. Indeed it may be said that the difference of sex is often a protection from such subtle vampirizations; because with the more normal attraction there simultaneously arises a corresponding hostility and repulsion; the sex-hate modifying the sex-love.

Regarding all this from the point of view not only of "morality" but of that nobler human emotion which we call

38

friendship, the question is bound to emerge at the end of it all;—is there actually in human nature such a thing as a pure love, a love, that is to say, entirely purged of the sex-element?

Are we to believe that now and again, though very rarely, there does arise out of some sub-sexual abyss in the soul a non-erotic emotion of adoration and tenderness, to which the same mysterious element responds from the soul of another? And is this, in rare and distinguished cases, nothing less than the magical harmony which we lightly call "friendship"?

If this *is* so, why then indeed there is an emotion in the world more powerful as well as more lasting than the thing which we know too well to be as deep as the grave and as cruel as the sea! But *is* there such an emotion?

None knoweth; save perhaps the heart of the friend! But if there is such an emotion, it is surely towards this, rather than towards any deepening of the sense of sin, that the imagination should move. Noble, self-sacrificing sex-love there undoubtedly is; but there come moments in one's life when even the most subliminated sex-feeling weighs upon us with the burden of a grand and monumental illusion. At such moments it were surely wise to pray to the great or the little gods to cause the up-flowing from some un-fathomable depths in the soul of that other feeling—that feeling which is not even a "sublimated" sex-emotion, which is not a sex-emotion at all—such as we perhaps hardly honour enough by calling it by the simple name of friendship!

And so the wheel comes full circle; and the issue of all the psychoanalytical learning in the world is found to be the inarticulate howl of the tent-maker of Tarsus: "Oh wretched man that I am! Who will deliver me from the body of this death!"

For what a thing it is, what a thing, this erotic mania of the human race! And no man has a right to say "would I were even as an animal or a bird, or a fish, or a tree, so that I were free of this bondage!" because the animals and

39

birds and fishes, and likely enough the trees and plants also, "groan and travail together" in the same tyranny. This thing is a force that lies behind every work of man's hands and every work of man's brain. The very energy with which we resist it is a sublimation of the thing we resist.

The mythological legends of the world imply that to nothing less than this thing the whole panorama of existence is due; and no amount of scientific analysis can separate it from the evolution of all organic life.

We speak of "the illusion of sex." Who can say whether, after all, it is not the unsexed moments that give us the false picture of the mystery of the world? Who can say whether the incredible glamour cast over everything by the sex-magic does not reveal the reality? Perhaps Nature *is* like that; and not as we see her in our less illuminated moods.

The thing must, at any rate, have inexhaustible creative power; for one knows well that the only cure for love-misery is in what we call "work"; and what, after all *is* "work" but a sort of diffused and depersonalized "love-making," orientated, through the identity-lust, towards the whole inanimate universe? It is this thing that gives to every rising of every sun its large and tremulous expectancy. It is this that gives to every frail and virginal new moon, carried like a torn white leaf upon the wind, its incurable ache of something beyond sorrow and beyond joy, like the cry, from across the verge, of an unborn child. It is this that gives to the familiar rain-sodden leaves in the autumnal cart-tracks their sudden unfamiliarity, their burden of things lifted up from unknown depths of memory, their sharp quick pang of heart-breaking thoughts.

It is this that strikes the hush upon us, terrible, wonderful, with a silence that is like the breath of a god, when in dead darkness under the great ash-trees we smell the very roots of the world. Soaked with this mystery and sobbing with the pulses of its quivering pressure the stirred green sap of all the vegetation of the earth yearns upward, yearns towards it knows not what; towards something that

40

transcends imagination. And when the Sea itself, the salt sterile Sea, is drawn in strange advancings and retreatings up and down the wet sand, is it possible not to think that something—an emanation, an effluence—from this universal power, is at work between those moonlit tides and their vampire cot-quean?

Psychoanalysis, at present, is only fumbling on the verge of these stupendous cosmic mysteries; but already, even in the short history of its explorations, what vistas have been opened up! For instance, when we mark the curious trick women have of closing their attempts to put some obscure matter, too subtle for man-made language, into articulate words, by a sudden gesture of the hand and the cry "like *that!*" or "like *this!*" one cannot help recognizing that the world is still waiting for a woman-psychoanalyst who will not confine herself to a tiresome repetition of the conclusions reached by men!

Why is it—one might ask these learned explorers—that, when two human beings meet and converse, they instinctively avoid looking, for more than a hurried moment, into one another's eyes? Is it a fear, an instinctive fear, of what one might incontinently stumble upon in those receding depths? Is it the sort of traditional avoidance, full of a recoiling shame, with which we turn from the sight of a person outrageously surprised? Is it that we would not willingly, or without warning, "uncover the nakedness" of a brother or a sister? When one considers what weird jungles, what marshes, what fens, what reedy swamps, the souls of men and women are, it may seem a perilous business to grope our way among one another!

What invitations, what rejections, what instinctive loathings, what furtive and indescribable attractions, we are bound to encounter as we go on our road! And what a veritable mad-house of invisible desires; desires to escape; desires to prevent escape; desires to destroy; desires to liberate; every family, every household, must present to the discerning eye! Psychoanalysis will indeed do something for the happiness of the race if it lays completely

41

bare the vortices of poisonous humours and evil feelings that swirl and seethe at the bottom of almost every family-life.

Why, for example, do young women, and indeed all unmarried women, suffer so abominably from "living at home"?

They love their parents. Their parents love them. They have amusements, interests, occupations; and yet they suffer a secret inexplicable anguish that is deeper than words can utter. Glib and unsympathetic moralists assure them that it is just "nerves." Religious teachers assure them that they are selfish little minxes, not to be happy at home with parents that love them so! They themselves are tormented by remorse; a remorse that only increases when they see their brothers happy and contented in an atmosphere that causes them a constant and incurable distress.

What is the explanation? May, it not be that while the tougher temperament of the male and his greater detachment from the ebb and flow of Nature's sub-rational tides protect him from this evil fatality, the magnetic receptivity of the female disarms her and renders her helpless in the presence of that mysterious and tragic cannibalism wherewith the most well-meaning parents devour, like Saturn, their defenceless offspring? The attitude of both parents, even under the happiest circumstances, when the appearance of a lover alleviates this deplorable strain, is something well worthy of psychoanalytical investigation and is often far less "moral," from a deeper point of view, than any overt sensual "sin."

The father is "jealous" of this young Perseus who would rescue his Andromeda from undeniable misery. And as for the mother, what a strange mixture of morbid vicarious pleasure combined with a furtive unbelievable irritation does that particular occasion drag into light!

Summing it all up, does not the final effect of any survey of psychoanalytical speculations leave the mind with a sense of the incredible richness and thickness of the world we live in? The further we analyze the depths of the human

42

situation the more vividly we become aware that in spite of the interaction between soul and body, what we are all really struggling to cope with are forces that are deeper than anything that could be called material. For, as the apostle says, "we are fighting" with more than flesh and blood; and "the mind, the mind, Master Shallow," is the arena of a drama whose stage ascends and descends into the workshops of the gods. Sex goes far and deep; but there come subterranean mental levels where the ordinary sex-struggle ceases; and yet where the eternal duality of good and evil does not cease.

Every human civilization as it rises and declines offers its own especial contribution to the gradual building up of authentic moral valuations; and the measure of the worth of the distinctions it makes is the measure of its lasting importance to humanity.

If the faltering and tentative speculations of psycho-analysis mean anything, as a lasting element in the moral contribution of our generation, they surely mean that evil has now become something very different from sin; some-thing different from sex-sensation; something different from sex-ecstasy. Evil, as far as we are concerned seems, when this great taboo has been lifted a little, to imply either cruelty or malice. Thus the tendency to cause suf-fering to others, under the hypocritical mask that it is "for their good," reveals itself as partaking far more clearly of the essence of evil than any kind of direct sensual pleasure, whether enjoyed for its own sake alone or enjoyed for the sake of mental curiosity.

And the psychoanalytical method when applied to every kind of moral indignation which has not cruelty or malice as its object, reveals that, hidden behind the ethical ges-ture, there is some sinister form of jealousy or some still more sinister form of the instinct to possess. How many human souls craving to taste for themselves the bitterness of the great salt-flood and to feel the splashing of the open sea and the sting of the free winds have been imprisoned by the ambiguous morality of others, until, with all hope gone,

43

they have rotted to death upon the sluggish wharf!

Human character is not rendered subtle and sensitive by external restraint. It is rendered subtle and sensitive, yes! and tender and pitiful too, by the experiences, beautiful or miserable, which it encounters in the tragic-comedy of its own unhampered fate.

The sex-instincts, as we have seen, are so closely associated with fear, so entwined with that strange and haunting fear of life and death and the unknown which waylays us at every turn, that only by a sane and happy manipulation of them can we look the universe in the face!

Moralistic "blague" bluffing so maliciously the tantalized souls of men and women, bids them take refuge in the anodyne of exhausting "work." But how deep a confession of failure is hidden in this imperative! What! Is the great world-spectacle of beauty and terror, revealed with every new awakening from sleep, aye! and following us into our very dreams, to be pruned and censored, to be "cabin'd' cribbed and confined," until it has no more significance than a phantasmal procession of fantastic puppets, wavering across a darkened stage?

Are we to make it the main purpose of our days to so drug ourselves with our work and our labor, that the incredible chance of our being conscious at all on this magical earth, is hardly realized until it is snatched away? If our natural humanity shrinks back in frightened horror at the formidable asceticism of the mediaeval saints, it must at least be acknowledged that now and then, in rare cases, some wonderful unearthly ecstasy substituted itself for what those saints renounced. Their desperate inhuman chastity might well be condemned as mad; but it had at least a tragic grandeur. The sort of drugged submission with which we so often submit to an ignoble prison-house has little in common with the astounding free-will of such suicidal heroism; but one can hardly refrain from associating even this excess of sacrifice, courageous though it may appear, with that awful sub-conscious terror which has haunted our race from the beginning.

44

It is as though, with most of us, we have only to give one hurried glance at the beauty and horror of the world, to be filled with an inextinguishable craving to seek refuge in the womb from which we sprang, the great nature-womb of negation and nihilism and non-life; and it is as a wretched substitute for such an escape that we wrap our race-conventions closely round us and drink the nepenthe of every taboo that gives us quietness and peace.

If it is really the case, as the psychoanalytical method seems to suggest, that our conviction of sex-sin in offering an escape from the world-fear only increases the world-fear, it is obvious that it darkens our consciousness of the vast possibilities of life. We are the creatures of strange unutterable impulses, super-human and sub-human, personal and impersonal. Every conscious soul stands hesitating and faltering on the verge of terrific half-realized powers, among which the imagination moves as an actual creator. Vast demoniac energies surge up within us from incredible gulfs; and our thoughts are penetrated by perpetual response to mysterious forces that reach backward through an infinite past, and forward to an obscure future. It is necessary to lift the whole problem of good and evil into a level beyond the level where sex-sensations are of primary importance, either to be indulged or to be suppressed. And because the great sex-taboo, in place of liberating us from this over-preoccupation with sex, increases and intensifies it, it is to the advantage of simple human happiness that this taboo should be criticized and analyzed if not modified and relaxed.

Intelligent analysis of the suppressing strain will do more than anything else to diminish the frequency of passional crime and so civilize and rationalize the erotic life of humanity. One of the worst evils of our present industrial system is that it destroys in the lives of so many any gracious or intelligent conception of what the meaning of life is.

Occupations and interests, altogether alien from the individual's personal response to the universe, are made so

45

exacting and so exhausting that there is hardly any margin left wherein a man can call his soul his own. And lacking the natural initiative of man, women fall hopelessly back upon those eternal sublimations of the sex-instinct that lead round and round in the same teasing and enclosed circle.

As soon as human beings come to recognize that it is as individuals possessed of vibrant senses and creative imaginations that they can alone fulfill their fate and colour it with thrilling colours, there will be a wide-spread revolt against all this misplacement of the centre of gravity. The nerves and senses are not jailers of the soul; neither are they caged wild beasts. They are gates and floodways through which the energies of the mind respond to the energies of the universe. It throws a very vivid light upon the whole problem when one compares what might be called the "marginal reaction"—by which I mean a person's response to the beauty and magic of things—of a taboo-ridden moralist of sound and strong character with that of a taboo-liberated individualist of unsound and weak character. Which of these two, when he comes to die, has known most of the tragic-comedy of life, has suffered most, has endured most, has been most intensely conscious and aware? Surely the latter! Surely the weak one! A great deal of harm to the cause of moral liberation has been done by the fact that the would-be liberators make so much of the "strong man" and the "strong woman." Strength too often is a mere popular nickname for insensibility. A heap of mud is "strong." The divine child in the arms of His mother is very "weak." Over and over again in the transactions of life one encounters a strong and malicious moralist engaged in cruelly persecuting some weak and sensitive nature whose ironical submission is its only retort.

The strong and the cunning are always able to take care of themselves; and they do take care of themselves under the present regime, which is admirably adapted to their shrewd hypocrisies. The would-be liberators, like Artzibasheff with his muscular and unscrupulous Sanine make a

46

grievous mistake. The brutal "Sanines" of our present life are just the ones that offer the best excuse for the most rigid restrictions. Indeed, if one was to be left at *their* mercy under any change, one would lament the breaking of the taboo. Darwin and Nietzsche with their ambiguous doctrine of the "survival of the fittest," the most wickedly misunderstood theory that has ever entered the brain of man, are not our wisest guides in this great revolution. Emerson, Ibsen, Carlyle, together with many vigorous writers of our day, carry on this worship of strength. What a relief to turn from these character-cultists to the infinite and magical tenderness of the Christian saints and their profound recognition of the eternal value of every human soul, "weak" or otherwise! What one dreads most of all in any possible change of attitude, is this very tyranny of the strong over the weak.

How foolishly the great Nietzsche summed up this subtle matter!

Was he blind and deaf to human psychology in those little hotels in Rapallo and Genoa, in Venice and Turin? Did he not see over and over again that the strong "well-constituted" one, in any human menage, is the one who maliciously and abominably persecutes with her "moral-ity" or with his "morality" the wretched weak one, whose marginal response to the beauty and terror of the universe is so much more vivid than his own? When the strong, clean, patient, dutiful, moral characters cease to be pos-sessive; when they really enter, with clairvoyant sym-pathy, into their "possessed" one's will to escape; when they become magnanimously self-effacing and genuinely philosophical; why, then, we may be driven to confess that the neurasthenic subjects of psychoanalysis are less deserv-ing of consideration than their saner companions! But until then we must continue to be "Christian"; in the sense of holding a brief for the "unfit." To retain the imag-inative sympathy of Christianity and the loyal tenderness of Christianity, while analyzing and relaxing its sex-taboo; *that*, rather than any encouragement of the brutality of the

47

"blond beast," is what our questionable civilization de-
mands. But it is a question whether we shall ever get it
until a wiser rhythm is struck between the human well-
being of the individual and the economic structure of
Society.

FIVE HUNDRED COPIES PRINTED

MARCH MCMXXIII

COPY NO.

CPSIA information can be obtained
at www.ICGtesting.com
Printed in the USA
BVHW041333220520
580136BV00011B/847